Moments of silence

ALBERT KRASSNER

MOMENTS OF SILENCE

Veridon Editions

Photographs by Mito Covarrubias

Moments of silence.
No utterances at all
Except to Oneself...

Poems by Albert Krassner

DEDICATION

To the wonders in Nature,
the differences and oneness
as it is for all persons
in all times
everywhere.

$35.00
ISBN 0-912061-14-6
Copyright 1987 by Albert Krassner
Graphic design: arcoiris/Mexico
All rights reserved
Veridon Editions
Box 65, Wykagyl Station
New Rochelle, NY 10804
USA

A PRAYER

☼ Lord,
let me fulfill my mission
however You guide me.

Let it be
May I go in ease to bring peace on earth,
whatever You wish it to be.
May I go in good health and in good fellowship
to do good.

May it be limited in controversy.
May it bring goodness and gladness to others.
May I go in ease to bring peace on earth,
goodwill to man.

☼ Whatever word is regularly used by anyone
that has reference to the Unknowable
but is experienced as a longing,
a feeling of love and peace and contentment
by which a human being
'knows' that there is something more.

PROLOGUE

MOMENTS OF SILENCE through poetic and photographic expressions
offers an opportunity to journey with the authors and perhaps harken
to what they have seen and felt and wished to share with others.
Theirs was discovery, sensing in silence and the generating space that it creates,
the continuum from the gross to the subtle, from images their echoes.
The book is a step in a process, again from gross to subtle.

The emphasis of the visuals is on space where it appears everything takes place,
thus the size of the photographs. Selecting what also appears to be relevant
indicates one particular stage; presenting it to others attempts to communicate
a personal discovery, perhaps useful to others.
The mixture of haiku and free poetry
- a measured discipline with a more contemporary way of expression -
is meant to convey the intention to be more in order with the laws of nature
as they are recognized and acknowledged.

The order of the presentation of the elements seemed to be
a natural progression ending with tribute to a guide
connecting the physical world and spiritual realm.
The treatment is of a flowing nature with accents here and there
to relieve the eye of spectacle wonders and to bring the mind to rest
on consideration of higher things. The images are impersonal,
everybody has seen them, the photographs only recreates them.
Neither size nor color is luxury,
in fact they are very modest compared to Nature.

The words are not new since the heart is very old.

CONTENTS

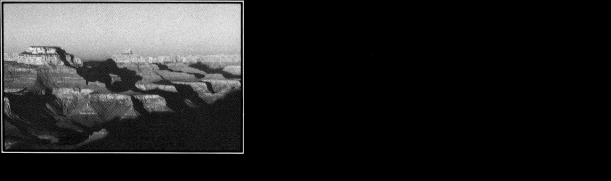

First moment
EARTH

God's revelations
Realized by man in man.
More so in nature.

Mountains will remain
Beyond my imagination
As infinity.

Having had its day
A dead tree just stands in place...
Nothing lasts forever.

Not seeking
Just being...

Not defining
All accepting...

No demanding
Faith expanding

Without knowing
On going...

Inner listening
Gladness - glistening.

A walk on a leaf-bedded trail,
sensing the beauty that is nature's way.
All around
the leaves have turned in recognition that their time has come
to make a grand exit... not just slip away to be unmissed.
The senses are aroused at the splendor of the reds,
golds and browns bathing in the warm sunlight
in a setting of a totally blue sky.
Nature is beaming today,
and her radiance reaches right through
to the recesses of the heart.

At peace with oneself
Feeling universal love...
No limitations.

Second moment
WATER

Capturing beauty
Not humanly possible.
Only to enjoy.

Constantly moving
The sea rolls and churns on top.
Always calm below.

My mind's thoughts rise like ocean waves
incessantly, never the same...

Always changing... different... but the

From the same source...
sometimes agitated... raging...
sometimes placid... clear... calm...
all powerful but affected by

Neither can be contained... I watch both

never... never... never...

same... in size... shape... different...

energy in different forms... water... thought...
running wild...
flowing gently...
wind... moon... word... another...

wonder... wonder... wonder...

Reviewing my thoughts
Following the endless flow.
Fascinating show.

Let it run
This feeling begun
Let it go
Wherever it may flow
Trust the way
Come what may
See it through
With God in view
No matter what comes
Accept all not some
Keeping the mind still
By the higher will
Ever and ever more
Feelings become more sure
Whatever it may be
This way to become more free.

Form or formless
Does not matter which it is
When it comes to God.

Third moment
FIRE

Seeing with a deeper I
Seeing with another eye
Seeing but not seeing like before
Seeing nothing but sensing more.
Sensing something else to be
Sensing with another part of me
Sensing - seeing - are the same
Both for perceiving in a different name.
Feeling generated from a view
Reactions happening inside of you.
The mind takes what it is told
It blows hot - it blows cold.
Thoughts are started - they come and go
All a part of an endless flow.
The mind will try to call the tune
Go here - go there - even to the moon.
The heart does see in another way
From it - all come into play.

Seeing nothingness
But seeing everything
All really worthwhile.

No matter what it is
There is always more to be seen
Appearing later.

Seeing miracle
Not recognizing its source.
So it is for some.

Undisturbed nature
Stimulating the eye... then thoughts
To see and not touch.

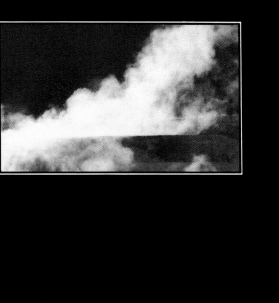

Fourth moment
AIR

The rustling of wind
The long silence in the air...
Stirring inner sounds.

Warm, windless air flows
Gentle sloping green vistas
Far away mountains.

Alone and lonely
So it is from time to time.
Such feelings arise.

To love is to live,
To love is to want to share,
To share with one
Or with many?

With one, there is aloneness,
But with no one, there is loneliness...
Fulfillment is the freedom,
To care and to compare,
To need and to give,
To seek and to deny,
To trust and to fear.

Strong winds blowing sounds
Intermittent wails of fury
Followed by silence.

Like wind in tree tops
Without seeing - believing ...
So it is with faith.

Outer facts happen
Beyond anyone's control.
Living continues.

Fifth moment
ETHER

Relief lies within
Truth and goodness never leave.
God never betrays.

Nature's majesty
Beyond understanding and time
To serve and be served.

Nothing is out there
Nothing outside anywhere
Only to be aware.

Nothing is apart
Created from One by One
This Truth to be won.

All is here and now
Nothing later nor before
No one keeping score.

Steadiness continues
Despite all appearances
For a man of faith.

Nature in command
Nothing anyone can do.
Vivid reminder.

Inspired...
wondering how it happened?
How did the thought arise -
a positive, exciting one...
Where did it come from?
It was somewhere, wasn't it?
Was there a guide... but where?

All part of the continuing process -
a new awareness - increasing wondering -
watching my thoughts - come and go -
being a viewer -
seeing that I am only a channel.

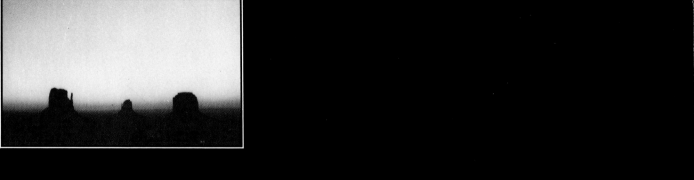

There was a guide.
There was for me.
Moments of silence
Being totally free.

Without any ego
It was in its place
Part of the All
An experience - grace.

How does one tell
How does one know
On whom to rely
With whom to go.

The test is simple
For one and all
It is never a personality
On whom to call.